Carpenters

by Debbie L. Yanuck

Consultant:
Fred Day
Director of School-To-Careers
Associated Builders and Contractors

Bridgestone Books
an imprint of Capstone Press
Mankato, Minnesota

Bridgestone Books are published by Capstone Press
151 Good Counsel Drive, P.O. Box 669, Mankato, Minnesota 56002
http://www.capstone-press.com

Library of Congress Cataloging-in-Publication Data
Yanuck, Debbie L.
    Carpenters/by Debbie L. Yanuck.
    p. cm.—(Community helpers)
    Includes bibliographical references and index.
    Summary: A simple introduction to what carpenters do, including where they work
and the tools they use.
    ISBN 0-7368-1126-5
    1. Carpentry—Juvenile literature. 2. Carpenters—Juvenile literature. [1. Carpentry.
2. Carpenters. 3. Occupations.] I. Title. II. Community helpers (Mankato, Minn.)
TH5607 .Y36 2002
694'.092—dc21   2001003327

Editorial Credits
Megan Schoeneberger, editor; Karen Risch, product planning editor; Linda Clavel, cover
    production designer; Katy Kudela, photo researcher

Photo Credits
Capstone Press/Gregg Andersen, 4, 6
EyeWire Images, 20
Index Stock Imagery/Gary Conner, 18
Mark E. Gibson/Photophile, 8, 10
Photo Network/Robert W. Ginn, 12
Pictor, 14
Shaffer Photography/James L. Shaffer, 16
Visuals Unlimited/Mark Gibson, cover

1 2 3 4 5 6 07 06 05 04 03 02

Table of Contents

Carpenters 5

What Carpenters Do 7

Types of Carpenters 9

Where Carpenters Work 11

Tools Carpenters Use 13

What Carpenters Wear 15

Carpenters and School 17

People Who Help Carpenters 19

How Carpenters Help Others 21

Hands On: Build a Raft 22

Words to Know 23

Read More 24

Internet Sites 24

Index 24

Carpenters

Carpenters are people who build. Some carpenters build houses, schools, and hospitals. Other carpenters build boats. Carpenters sometimes remodel houses. They may add one room or fix the entire house. They also might put in new doors and windows.

remodel
to make a change to the shape or look of a building

5

What Carpenters Do

Carpenters do many jobs. They buy wood. They make sure the wood is not split or crooked. Carpenters read plans called blueprints. Blueprints show how to do a project. Carpenters then cut and shape the wood. They put the wood together with nails, screws, or glue.

blueprint
a plan for a building project

Types of Carpenters

Carpenters work on different projects. Rough carpenters make the frame for walls and roofs. They then build a house or building over the frame. Finish carpenters add trim around doors, walls, and windows.

trim
woodwork used around edges in buildings

Where Carpenters Work

Carpenters build where they are needed. Most carpenters work where buildings are being built. They move to another workplace when the job is done. They often work outdoors. Finish carpenters work indoors in new buildings or remodeled houses.

Tools Carpenters Use

Carpenters use many tools. They measure boards with tape measures. They use power saws and hand saws to cut wood. Carpenters smooth rough edges on wood with sandpaper. Carpenters use hammers or power nailers to drive nails into wood.

What Carpenters Wear

Carpenters wear gear to keep them safe. They wear goggles to keep wood chips out of their eyes. They often wear hard hats and boots with steel toes. These items keep carpenters from being hurt by falling objects. Carpenters wear tool belts that hold tools such as hammers.

goggles
glasses that protect a person's eyes

Carpenters and School

Carpenters learn to build in many ways. Some carpenters become apprentices. An apprentice learns by working with a skilled carpenter. Carpenters also learn at trade schools. Trade schools teach carpenters how to use power tools and read blueprints.

People Who Help Carpenters

Carpenters need other people to help them. Architects draw blueprints for the buildings. Plumbers put in pipes for running water. Electricians hook up wires so the buildings have electricity. Inspectors check that the buildings are built safely.

architect
a person who designs buildings

How Carpenters Help Others

Carpenters help build communities. They build houses where families live. They can make old houses look new again. Carpenters help build schools and hospitals.

Hands On: Build a Raft

Carpenters use wood to build. They sometimes use glue to hold the wood together. You can be a carpenter and build a raft.

What You Need

Craft sticks
Wood glue

What You Do

1. Place about 15 craft sticks next to each other side by side. The sticks should make a square.
2. Glue a craft stick along the top and bottom of the square to hold the sticks together.
3. Now glue one craft stick at an angle across the craft sticks. It will look like a letter "Z" across the top of the square.
4. Let the glue dry.

See if the raft will float in a sink or bathtub. Can you think of anything else you can build with your craft sticks?

Words to Know

apprentice (uh-PREN-tiss)—someone who learns a trade by working with a skilled person

blueprint (BLOO-print)—a plan for a building project

electrician (e-lek-TRISH-uhn)—someone who installs and fixes electrical items

frame (FRAYM)—the basic shape over which a house is built

inspector (in-SPEK-tur)—someone who checks or examines projects; inspectors make sure new buildings are safe.

plumber (PLUHM-ur)—someone who puts in pipes or repairs pipes for sinks, toilets, showers, and bathtubs

trade school (TRADE SKOOL)—a place where a person learns to do a job

Read More

Brown, Angela McHaney. *Carpenter.* Workers You Know. Austin, Texas: Raintree Steck-Vaughn, 2000.

Burby, Liza N. *A Day in the Life of a Carpenter.* The Kids' Career Library. New York: PowerKids Press, 1999.

Franchino, Vicky. *Carpenters.* Community Workers. Minneapolis: Compass Point Books, 2000.

Internet Sites

BLS Career Information—Carpenter
http://www.bls.gov/k12/html/gym_006.htm
What Does a Carpenter Do?
http://www.whatdotheydo.com/carpentr.htm

Index

apprentice, 17
blueprints, 7, 17, 19
boats, 5
boots, 15
finish carpenters, 9, 11
frame, 9
goggles, 15
hard hats, 15

hospitals, 5, 21
house, 5, 9, 11, 21
rough carpenters, 9
schools, 5, 21
tool belts, 15
tools, 13, 15, 17
trade schools, 17
wood, 7, 13